BRITAIN'S RAILWAYS IN TRANSITION 1976–90

John Evans

AMBERLEY

First published 2019

Amberley Publishing
The Hill, Stroud
Gloucestershire, GL5 4EP

www.amberley-books.com

Copyright © John Evans, 2019

The right of John Evans to be identified as the
Author of this work has been asserted in accordance
with the Copyrights, Designs and Patents Act 1988.

ISBN 978 1 4456 8267 9 (print)
ISBN 978 1 4456 8268 6 (ebook)

British Library Cataloguing in Publication Data.
A catalogue record for this book is available from
the British Library.

Typeset in 10pt on 13pt Celeste.
Origination by Amberley Publishing.
Printed in the UK.

The Good Old Days?

The volunteer gardener at Mytholmroyd station, near my home in the Calder Valley, looked up from the pansies he was planting and remembered the good old days. Well maybe, he conceded, they weren't *that* good.

'Yer didn't want to 'ang around here in the 1980s lad,' he said. 'Especially after dark. An 'aven for troublemakers.'

Today I use the station regularly at all times of day and always feel safe. Over the years it has lost its freight yard, staff, booking office, half the length of its platforms and its station buildings. But for a modest village station, it has a pretty intensive train service. It's also busy all day – and the flower beds look lovely. They are even restoring the long-redundant booking hall for community use. Welcome to the modern railway.

The story of Mytholmroyd mirrors that of so many stations that managed to survive the traumas of the 1960s. Just because Dr Beeching had moved on, the decline was hardly arrested. It was fascinating as an enthusiast to watch the railway in phase two of its transition. A legion of rail fans who never knew the exit of steam watched with the same melancholy eyes as the last 'Western' and 'Deltic' diesels surrendered to the arrival of the inevitable omnipotence of HSTs and Class 47 locomotives. One of the first photographs I took in 1976, when this survey starts, shows a diesel shunter trundling a long freight through Wigston, near Leicester, in a scene complete with endless sidings, telegraph poles, semaphore signals and wagons galore. It was the old railway clinging to life. By 1990 it seemed everything that made a railway interesting to the enthusiast had gone. Yet two days ago I was at Doncaster and counted thirty enthusiasts on a weekday paying homage to the modern railway. Long may it continue.

Any book of this kind cannot depict the whole of the railway scene during those fifteen years. My goal has been to record and illustrate some of the most important highlights and to indicate how things changed. A comparison between that diesel shunter at Wigston and *Yeoman Enterprise* on a private freight eleven years later is one example. I also touch on the growing heritage and main-line steam scene. Choosing what to include has been difficult, but in the end I decided on three categories – BR locomotive developments, changes to the way British Rail was working and preservation. Hopefully those who remember this period, and those who want to discover more about what happened, will find enough to interest them.

The late 1970s and 1980s will be remembered as a time of turmoil for this country. We saw punk rock, Thatcher versus Scargill, hyperinflation and ruinous industrial conflict. Against a background of economic and cultural instability, our railways saw revived demand and started to rise from the ashes of contraction that had been the 1960s. It was a legacy that lasted years. In 1997 I was on a management course with a senior executive from Midland Mainline, who had recently won the franchise to operate passenger trains out of St Pancras. I asked him about the issues he was facing.

'The railway of today is about customer service in a way it never was in the 1980s,' he said. 'But how do we re-train someone who spent most of their working life in a freight yard to deliver exemplary service to demanding customers?' The multitude of staff inherited from BR could hardly be dispensed with, he added.

During the 1980s, I was pursuing a career, getting married and involving myself in other distractions when a solemn devotion to the railway was clearly required. My thanks therefore go to Tony Woof, Bob Mullins, Richard Denny and Gordon Edgar, whose photographs have filled in some crucial gaps for me. Photographs not credited are my own. Once again my wife kindly proofread the text for me – she must be an expert after five books!

John Evans
Luddenden, West Yorkshire

The Search for a New Railway

After the storm came the calm. The tumultuous ten years from 1965 to 1975 relayed in the first volume of *British Railways in Transition* (Amberley Publishing, 2017) left a railway system searching for a new identity. British Rail had said farewell to its last steam engines (with three narrow gauge exceptions) and *The Reshaping of British Railways* administered by Dr Beeching was over, save for a handful of delayed closures. What lay ahead?

It was a time of endings and beginnings – a time when everyone knew there should be rapid progress towards a modern railway, but no one could see clearly how to get there. The years covered by this volume are set against a background of frightening instability. Rail unions – make that *all* unions – went on strike at the drop of a hat. Inflation soared to a heady 18 per cent in 1980. Government subsidies were all over the place. The number of passengers travelling by rail declined steadily throughout the early 1970s, reaching a low point in the early 1980s. It has since continued to rise, currently far exceeding the halcyon days around the turn of the twentieth century, before car travel was established.

What about the stations and other infrastructure? One thing we can learn from a study of Britain's railway stations is that they are in many cases transitory. A surprisingly large number of stations were closed in the nineteenth century and throughout the twentieth, and although there was a big spike in closures in the 1960s, they continued at a lower level over the next few decades until, gradually, re-openings became much more common, largely thanks to the input of local authorities (and heritage railways, but that is hardly the same thing). The continuing closures were for various reasons. Clayton West in Yorkshire was run down and finally closed in 1983; Radipole Halt in Weymouth went the following year due to unsafe wooden platforms. Others were rebuilt as cheaply as possible when repairs became due, often with feeble waiting shelters.

It was also the age of sectors for passenger traffic and freight, as the 1980s witnessed a worrying decline in goods traffic. In a bid to stem this problem, British Rail moved away from wagonloads and into more containers. Chairman Sir Bob Reid talked about BR becoming a business-led railway, which resulted in the closure of marshalling yards and the end of freight services being provided at many stations. Unable to compete with the cost of road haulage, rail freight looked doomed. Although coal traffic was also facing a downturn as pits closed, the introduction of merry-go-round trains provided a more user-friendly way of shifting loads from pit to power station. Much more prophetic was the introduction by Foster Yeoman of its own stone and aggregate trains, foreshadowing the privatisation that was to follow in the 1990s.

The 1980s marked the beginning of the revival of our railways. Ignoring those re-opened by heritage lines, some forty-five stations were brought back to life in the years from 1976 to 1990, starting a trend that continues to this day. This includes those on the Settle–Carlisle line, which had closed in 1970, and some others that had been closed for many years, such as Dunston-on-Tyne, which had been shut for nearly sixty years. Paisley Canal, in Renfrewshire, was closed for just seven years, but it was long enough for the site to be sold off, necessitating the construction of a completely new station a short distance away. Other stations lost their buildings and became unstaffed halts. Some – including huge stations like London Broad Street and Liverpool Exchange – were closed completely.

The creation of the Passenger Transport Authorities (later Passenger Transport Executives) between 1969 and local government re-organisation in 1974 had a far-reaching effect on the nation's passenger train services. At last we had bodies with a mandate to set passenger transport policy, and during the period covered by this book they got into their stride. In many cases, contraction of passenger services was arrested and old stations re-opened.

The look of the railway changed completely. Gone were telegraph poles, sidings at every station, semaphore signals and neat and tidy embankments. In their place were overhead catenaries as electrification progressed as fast as cash would allow, colour light signals and lots of those electrical boxes that suddenly appeared all over the railway system, often with graffiti to decorate them. It was the last decade when efforts were made to contain lineside undergrowth. Sometimes these days it seems like you are travelling through a tunnel of trees, but lurking underneath is actually a cutting or an embankment.

Blue is the Colour

The new, post-steam identity initially appeared visually as station name boards in an elegant lower case font; locomotives and suburban multiple units were painted plain Monastral blue with full yellow warning panels and passenger rolling stock in blue and light grey. It also included the double arrow symbol, which continues to this day as the corporate identity to signify a railway station. In 1976, when this study commences, there were still a few engines around painted green and varied opinions exist about which was the very last engine to finally appear in Rail blue. It's one of those items of minutiae that enthusiasts love to debate. According to a colleague, the last one was Class 20 No. 20141, which was still green in early 1980. Certainly one of the last was Class 40 No. 40106, which was painted Rail blue at Crewe in September 1978, but was immediately repainted green for its role as a celebrity engine.

If the move to the new livery proceeded slowly, then the application of TOPS numbers had advanced fairly swiftly in 1973 and 1974. A few, such as the dwindling number of 'Western' Class 52 engines and the Brush *Falcon*, never received TOPS numbers. Some Class 45 engines also entered 1976 with their original numbers as BR sorted out the future classification of individual locomotives.

Having created a new railway based on a very rigid corporate identity with clear and familiar signage and plain blue locomotives and diesel units, British Rail lost its way completely in the 1980s. Instead of updating the blue livery, or replacing it with something new, it suddenly seemed it was a case of anything goes. It was possible to see a Class 47 in at least six different liveries, including Great Western Brunswick Green and LNER apple green. The 1987 issues of *Motive Power Pocket Book* illustrate no fewer than thirteen different BR liveries, including three Railfreight designs, updated versions of Monastral blue, Network SouthEast and ScotRail with both blue and red stripes, and many others. The result was that many trains sported a complete mixture of colours and you could see a Network SouthEast train at Exeter in the West Country pulling a train with three different colours of rolling stock.

In 1982, the recently appointed chief executive of British Rail, Bob Reid, presided over huge changes to the railway system. They included new accounting systems and the division of the railway into five business sectors. A sceptical Conservative government wanted wholesale improvements to how the railways were run, which led to cuts in costs and staff numbers (and, eventually, privatisation). The balance sheet was buoyed by a much stronger economy. BR as the butt of endless jokes about curly sandwiches was not appropriate anymore (if you wanted Britain's best breakfast, try that served on the early morning service from Coventry to Euston!). Things were on the up.

Diesels in Detail

The years 1976 to 1990 saw the end of a strategic blunder. This was the decision to allow individual regions to order their own diesel locomotives. Quite how this came about is unclear, but BR's management wanted to see how hydraulic transmission and high-speed lightweight diesel engines would compare with low-speed diesels and electric transmission. Allowing the Western Region to order more than 360 hydraulic engines, however, hardly constitutes a comparative trial. When British Railways was formed in 1948, a halt was quickly placed on new orders of any steam locomotives except those of the new BR Standard designs (excepting five dock tanks). Why such a marked change in policy a few years later? As the first of these not-so-old warriors went quickly to the scrapyard, hardly a tear was shed. Only the later, successful Hymek and the 'Western' Class 52, with its handsome body design, created significant emotion.

When a fund was set up to rescue pioneer diesel D601 *Ark Royal* from Barry scrapyard in the 1980s, it failed. Enthusiasts, it seemed, were happy to subscribe to endless rusty 'Hall' Class steam locomotives from Barry scrapyard and five redundant 'Deltics' (with both the prototype and one other in the National Collection), but not an obsolete, but rather intriguing, Class 41 'Warship'.

The size of the locomotive fleet contracted sharply between 1976 and 1990. During those fifteen years, some 42 per cent of BR locomotives were withdrawn.

Year	Size of diesel fleet (number of classes)	Size of electric fleet (number of classes)	Total
1976	3,435 (25)	442 (11)	3,877 (36)
1978	3,283 (23)	276 (9)	3,559 (32)
1984	3,152 (18)	243 (7)	3,395 (25)
1986	2,240 (16)	240 (7)	2,480 (23)
1990	1,813 (14)	269 (8)	2,259 (22)

There were some notable casualties. These included enthusiast favourites like the 'Western' and 'Deltic' diesels; the more successful of the pilot scheme types, like the Class 24 and 25 Type 2 engines; the weighty Class 40 and 45 Type 4s; and a whole raft of diesel shunters as their work dried up. This table shows the demise of the types earmarked for withdrawal after 1975, with twenty of the thirty-six types of locomotive then in service failing to survive until 1990.

BR Class	Type	Power Unit	Introduced	Total built	Withdrawal completed
Class 01	0-4-0	Diesel	1956	4	1981
Class 05	0-6-0	Diesel	1955	69	1981
Class 06	0-4-0	Diesel	1958	35	1981
Class 07	0-6-0	Diesel	1962	14	1977
Class 13	0-6-0+0-6-0	Diesel	Rebuilt 1965	3	1986
Class 24	Bo-Bo	Diesel	1958	151	1980
Class 25	Bo-Bo	Diesel	1961	327	1987
Class 27	Bo-Bo	Diesel	1961	69	1987
Class 40	1Co-Co1	Diesel	1958	200	1985
Class 44	1Co-Co1	Diesel	1959	10	1980
Class 45	1Co-Co1	Diesel	1960	127	1989
Class 46	1Co-Co1	Diesel	1961	56	1984
Class 52	C-C	Diesel	1961	74	1977
Class 55	Co-Co	Diesel	1961	22	1981
Class 71	Bo-Bo	DC Electric	1958	24	1977
Class 74	Bo-Bo	Electro-Diesel	Rebuilt 1967	10	1977
Class 76	Bo-Bo	DC Electric	1941	58	1981
Class 82	Bo-Bo	AC Electric	1960	10	1987
Class 83	Bo-Bo	AC Electric	1960	15	1989
Class 84	Bo-Bo	AC Electric	1960	10	1980

Most withdrawals were due to the advent of more modern motive power, the decline in freight traffic, electrification, basic obsolescence, high running or maintenance costs or simply being non-standard. Quite a few were uneconomical to repair after accidents. In the case of the single Class 05 Barclay shunter, it was retained to work on the Isle of Wight, and even after withdrawal from capital stock in 1981 it was used for four more years as a departmental engine. In contrast, the Class 74 electro-diesel seemed a good idea for utilising redundant Class 71 electric locomotives, but in practice the Class 74 was fraught with problems when running with diesel power and the boat train services they were designed to haul were in decline.

The early BR diesels, ordered in large numbers off the drawing board, suffered from the rapid march of progress. D1, delivered in 1959 and later to become Class 44, developed 2,300 bhp and weighed a mighty 133 tons. D1500, later Class 47, was built three years later with the same engine uprated to 2,750 bhp. But the designers shaved 16 tons off the engine's weight, all of which D1's power unit had to shift before anything was hung on the coupling. It is no surprise that the later locomotive was considered so much better.

Too Much Choice?

Writing in 1964, the editor of *Locospotters' Annual* gave a very erudite analysis of some of BR's motive power issues, saying that the English Electric Type 4 (Class 40) had been found after a few weeks' use by the Eastern Region to be 'no more than the equal in haulage and speed capability of a Pacific steam locomotive in first-class condition'. Several reports from the London Midland Region assessed the same engines as 'about as good as a rebuilt Royal Scot'. In each case, the Class 40 was a stopgap before electrification. This went ahead as planned on the lines out of Euston. Under the original Modernisation Plan of 1955, electrification of the King's Cross to York and Leeds route was also seen as a priority; when this was shelved, the Eastern Region wanted a locomotive that would be an effective substitute in delivering regular 100 mph performance. This led to the order of the expensive and complicated 'Deltic' locomotives, which had two eighteen-cylinder power units, but even so weighed only 100 tons. After the inevitable teething troubles, they settled down to deliver a much higher level of performance than other BR passenger diesels, and continued the East Coast route's reputation for fast running. The introduction of the High Speed Trains put the future of the 'Deltics' in jeopardy, but they gave twenty years of service followed by a great fanfare when they were withdrawn.

The shape of the 1970s and 1980s locomotive fleet was determined in other ways. The Western Region soon decided it did not need Type 2 engines at all and focused on Type 3s (initially Hymeks and then English Electric Class 37s). The region said a Type 2 was simply not the equivalent of a 'Grange' or 'Hall' steam 4-6-0. The London Midland ordered no Type 3s, but found a big fleet of Type 2s (Sulzer Classes 24 and 25) suited its needs and could be used in multiple for more power. The Eastern and North Eastern Regions wanted Types 2, 3, 4 and 5 for different tasks. The Scottish Region used Type 2s, often in multiple. And everyone thought the very first production main-line diesel, the Class 20, was a good idea.

So there we have the background to British Railways motive power in 1976. At that time, it was basically the old railway without steam. What we might call 'phase two' of the new railway occurred during the next fifteen years. The game changer in the case of passenger locomotives was the addition of nearly 200 HST power cars and their trains, plus many multiple units, both diesel and electric, quite a few of which are still in service at the time of writing. These include Class 313, 507, 508 and many Pacers, Sprinters and Express units.

The growing importance of multiple unit-type trains and the success of the first General Motors motive power (Class 59) gave industry watchers in 1990 a strong clue about the kind of railway that lay ahead, and indeed, the one we use today. More power for bulk freight trains was essential. New Type 5 diesels had been ordered for this task, but issues with BR's own Class 56 and 58 heavy haulers opened a void that General Motors quietly filled with its Class 59 and 66 locomotives.

While the nationalised system was going through an endless series of traumas, new heritage railways were springing up like golden daffodils round a village road sign. Today there are around seventy standard gauge lines, most of which went through their gestation period between 1976 and 1990. Initially aimed at enthusiasts, they soon became essential tourist attractions. One of the more bizarre occurrences during the period under review was a plan by the local authority in Bradford to open its own tourist railway, providing unwanted competition for the nearby Keighley and Worth Valley line, which had worked tirelessly to create a major tourist attraction of benefit to the Bradford City Council area. Quite why a council should think they could create a heritage railway when even British Railways was handing over the Vale of Rheidol line to enthusiasts is baffling. A few of these schemes fell by the wayside, but most thrived and are with us today. In addition to those lines, there are dozens of steam centres, miniature and park railways and the important narrow-gauge lines. Among these, the achievement of the Ffestiniog Railway in rebuilding back to Blaenau Ffestiniog has to be the highlight.

At the end of 1975, there were seventeen standard-gauge tourist railways – lines that actually ran a regular service of more than a mile, usually on ex-BR routes. Most of those had opened in the 1970s. By 1990 this number had increased to thirty-seven, the new arrivals including some very well-known operations, such as the Llangollen Railway, the Gloucestershire Warwickshire Railway, the Mid Hants Railway and the Swanage Railway. Depending on how the numbers are calculated, there are around ninety heritage lines operating today.

New Stars

The success of main-line steam excursions, which had begun tentatively in 1971, moved swiftly forward. The BR stance against steam seemed almost to have never happened. BR were soon running their own steam trains using privately preserved locomotives and making a good job of it. This incentivised an increasing number of locomotive owners to take their engines on the main line and there were some notable stars. Who can forget the scepticism that greeted the prospect of an un-rebuilt Bulleid light Pacific tackling Ais Gill? And who can forget how effectively No. 34092 *City of Wells* answered those doubts? Even that rustiest of hulks, and a ludicrous proposition for preservation, No. 71000 *Duke of Gloucester,* was back at work and performing rather better than it had when BR owned it. Possibly the two most inspirational engines to return to steam in the 1980s were *Duchess of Hamilton* and *Mallard,* paving the way for many other static giants to exercise their prowess once again. The passion for steam railways was something that could not be ignored, although the demands for private diesel locomotives to receive similar treatment were firmly resisted.

The Wonder of Woodhams

Fortunately the preservation scene had an unlikely hero in a genial Welshman named Dai Woodham, whose scrapyard at Barry in South Wales full of condemned BR steam engines has become a tale worthy of folklore. Without his yard, we would have had a poor selection of locomotives in preservation, and those seventy steam railways, if created, would have been forced to use small industrial types. These are neither as suitable nor quite as interesting as the bigger BR engines.

For quite a few years I lived in California and was a tour guide at a Los Angeles railway museum. We were trying to find a way of overhauling a tiny Southern Pacific 0-4-0ST (surely the smallest steam locomotive in the USA) but could not raise the funds nor find anyone to overhaul the boiler. When I mentioned to my museum colleagues that, in the UK, some 200 scrap steam engines had been rescued in twenty years and half of them were back at work – including many on the main line – they could not believe it. We may be guilty of underestimating our passion for heritage railways in this country and the skills and infrastructure we have created.

That new industry was created in the 1970s and 1980s. It was soon clear that engines that were declared impossible to restore in 1973 would be purchased eagerly ten years later. It is probably fair to say that there is no such thing as a locomotive that cannot be restored, given the right amount of funding. Over the twenty-three years that locomotives were rescued from Barry, 1981 was the busiest, with twenty-one departures. In 1977, only one engine, 4F 0-6-0 No. 44422, left the yard. In all, 150 locomotives were saved during the period from 1976 to 1990. In some cases a wreck became a gleaming beacon of steam in only a couple of years.

The diesel preservation movement eventually got into its stride. Having lost the chance to acquire some of the first pioneering locomotives, enthusiasts moved swiftly and effectively to save examples of their favourite engines as the 1980s saw a major rationalisation of types in service. Thus, 'Deltics', 'Westerns', Class 40s and 45s, plus many smaller types and shunters found their way to preservation centres. As already mentioned, one key problem for preservationists was British Rail's adamantly defiant attitude to running heritage diesels on their lines. Looking back this seems increasingly odd – they would allow a steam engine that may have endured fifteen years rusting in the salt-laden air at Barry to operate, but not a diesel that had spent its whole life in their own care.

Year by Year

What follows is a story in words and pictures of those years. It follows on in the same style as *British Railways in Transition 1965–75*, which seemed to prove popular. Hopefully these memories and pictures will re-awaken, or introduce you for the first time, to a period in railway history that was often frustrating and often confusing, but always fascinating.

1976

The first three Class 40s are taken out of service. No. 44003 *Skiddaw* is the first Class 44 to be withdrawn. Class 87 No. 87001 is named *Stephenson*. The first Brush Type 2, No. 31001, is withdrawn for preservation. The prototype PEP electric multiple unit, No. 920001, starts trials in Glasgow. Some locomotives are having their headcode panels replaced with two marker lights, No. 45071 being one of the first. Class 312 electric multiple units for the West Midlands and the Eastern Region are unveiled. The unique Brush *Falcon* locomotive arrives at Cashmore's scrapyard for breaking up.

While West Midlands PTE announces new services, Merseyside PTE proposes cuts, including eliminating the Birkenhead to Wrexham diesel multiple unit service. Half of the 'Western' class remaining in service are withdrawn at the end of the year, with just seven left in action. A few Gresley buffet cars are still in use and the Great Western Society's vintage train appears on rail tours. Work has started on building a new maintenance depot at Penzance. The bridge carrying the closed Bedford–Cambridge route over the East Coast Main Line is demolished. Britain's heaviest freight train starts running, with three Class 37s hauling 3,000 tons of iron ore in Wales. The Great Northern inner suburban electric service commences, using Class 313 units. All the Class 71 electric locomotives go into store. New Class 253 HST trains transform schedules on the Western Region with regular 125-mph trains running. At the end of the year, 136 locomotives, mainly shunters, remain in green livery.

A new heritage railway opens, the West Somerset, linking Minehead and Blue Anchor. The Great Central launches a share appeal to buy the line, and preservationists start restoring the station buildings at Swanage. The Gloucestershire Warwickshire Railway Society announces ambitious plans to save the disused Cheltenham to Stratford-upon-Avon line. The proposed East Somerset Railway buys Cranmore station. The Talyllyn Railway opens an extension to Nant Gwernol. Magdalen Road station in Norfolk is under threat of closure, having only been re-opened in 1975 (it survives today as Watlington).

A number of bombs, attributed to the IRA, explode on trains. London Transport announces a 23 per cent train fare rise, and 29 per cent for season tickets. The Queen visits Wolverton Works to see the new Royal Train. BR says the future of the Woodhead route is under review as it needs £3 million of rectification work.

The only Eastern Region engine at Barry scrapyard, B1 No. 61264, departs for preservation, leaving about 150 steam locomotives remaining. Nos. 6000 *King George V*, 6201 *Princess Elizabeth* and 35028 *Clan Line* are based at Bulmers, Hereford, for the 1976 season of rail tours. Duchess Pacific No. 6229 *Duchess of Hamilton* is being restored at Swindon for the National Railway Museum. It was previously at Butlins Holiday Camp in Minehead on display. A fund set up to preserve a Class 24 is said to be the first for a diesel locomotive in the UK.

1977

After much fanfare and many farewell trips, the last Class 52 'Western' diesels are withdrawn, with seven being preserved. Routine withdrawals of Class 26s and 46s start. The first Class 56, No. 56006, enters service after several months of remedial work since it was built in Romania. The frame of No. 56031, the first British-built example of this class, is laid down at Doncaster. Two Stratford-based Class 47s are painted with Union Flags to mark the Queen's Silver Jubilee. No. 84007 becomes the first West Coast AC electric locomotive to be withdrawn, excepting those damaged by fire or accidents. The last surviving Class 74 electro-diesel is withdrawn, the end of a short-lived and unsuccessful conversion. A number of Swindon InterCity units have been transferred to work on Trans-Pennine services. Some Class 31s are repainted with white bands. The name *Stephenson* has been transferred from No. 87001 to No. 87101 as BR wish to have a dedicated set of names for the Class 87s. No. 87001 has now become *Royal Scot*. The first HST set for the Eastern Region, No. 254001, is delivered. For twelve months, the Eastern Region runs a titled train called the Silver Jubilee between King's Cross and Edinburgh to mark twenty-five years of the Queen being on the throne.

Liverpool Exchange is closed and partly replaced by Moorfields underground station. Leicester station is to be rebuilt, Wigan Wallgate is modernised and a new station at Gloucester is opened. The well-known bridge across the Taw Estuary at Barnstaple is demolished. Consideration is being given to withdrawing passenger services between Halifax and Todmorden. The Braintree branch is electrified and the Rail Report for 1977 shows increasing passenger numbers and reduced losses on freight. Brinnington station in Stockport is opened. BR is promoting wagonload freight services under the name Speedlink. Newton Aycliffe station in County Durham is opened while Birmingham Snow Hill station, in a very poor state since closure to rail services in 1968 and used since then as a car park, is demolished. The Queen travels by train on her Silver Jubilee tour of Britain.

The Peak Railway Society, which wants to re-open the line from Matlock to Buxton, takes a lease on Matlock station buildings. Class EM1 electric locomotive No. 76020 is acquired by the National Railway Museum, while a fund set up to preserve D601 *Ark Royal* from Barry scrapyard fails due to a lack of support. 'Castle' class 4-6-0 No. 4079 *Pendennis Castle* is sold to a company in Australia. Five summer steam specials are cancelled through a lack of bookings. The last fireless locomotive at work, at Gravesend Paper Mill, is retired. New homes are found for a group of National Collection locomotives that have been in store for many years, including Q1 0-6-0 No. 33001, an M7, Class 5 No. 45000 and 4-6-0 No. 30850 *Lord Nelson*. Great Northern Railway 4-4-2 No. 990 *Henry Oakley* is returned to work at the Keighley & Worth Valley Railway. The railway also announced the purchase of an S160 2-8-0 from Poland. The Mid-Hants heritage railway opens between Alresford and Ropley, as does the Nene Valley Railway near Peterborough.

1978

New Class 507 electric multiple units are delivered from York to Merseyrail. After thirteen years, BR decides to relax the plain Monastral blue livery and experimentally paints a new freight locomotive, No. 56036, in a large logo style, exhibiting it at several open days. 'Western' D1041 *Western Prince* is acquired for preservation and it's the last run of the 'Yorkshire Pullman'. Class 40 No. 40106 gets a new coat of green paint, an early chink in the armour of overall blue. With all Class 87s named, a start is made on Class 86 and No. 86101 is named *Sir William A. Stanier F.R.S.*, sponsored by the Locomotive Club of Great Britain. Three Class 15 engines are moved to Colchester as heating units. At a time of weeding out non-standard shunters, the Class 06 engines are mostly still at work in Scotland, while No. 01002 is kept busy at Holyhead breakwater (still carrying its pre-1956 lion and wheel emblem). An oddity seen on an excursion is hump shunter No. 13003. The first ATP-P pre-production vehicle, No. 370001, is presented to the media. Its new livery will later be used for BR's InterCity locomotives and coaches. Class 55s start to lose their East Coast work to the new HSTs and rail fans follow the last few Class 24, 44 and 84 locomotives at work with intense interest. Steam is still at work at Bold Colliery in Lancashire. There are still six Pullman camping coaches at Marazion station in Cornwall. Class 40 and 47 locomotives have taken over most services on the Highland main line. The first Class 50 to be named is No. 50035 *Ark Royal*.

Rail fares rise by a mighty 15 per cent. To cope with new HST trains and also heavy stone trains from Merehead Quarry, the layout at Westbury is remodelled. The East Coast route loses its last semaphore signals. Wadebridge freight depot in Cornwall closes, but a new station at Bedford Midland opens. Six Stratford-based Class 47s are named and a new society plans to re-open the King's Lynn to Hunstanton line (which never happens). A dramatic cable-stayed bridge is constructed to carry the Virginia Water to Weybridge line over the new M25 motorway. One of the greatest railway photographers, Bishop Eric Treacy, dies. Hunts Back in Manchester, once the most prestigious railway office in the north, is demolished. It was opposite Victoria station.

The Ffestiniog Railway's deviation reaches Tanygrisiau, not far from the eventual terminus at Blaenau. Two extra steam locomotives back at work are Nos 6115 *Scots Guardsman* and 70000 *Britannia*. The Gwili Railway re-opens 1 mile of track at Bronwydd Arms in Wales. An action committee announces it plans to re-open the Wymondham to Dereham branch.

1979

The 'Cornish Riviera' and 'Golden Hind' expresses switch to HST units. Electric locomotive E5001 goes on display at the National Railway Museum. Crewe starts rebuilding Class 47s as push-pull variants for the Edinburgh to Glasgow service and classes them as 47/7. Meanwhile, No. 47601, fitted with a Class 56 engine, is rebuilt with a Class 58 engine and renumbered 47901. The APT-P is now a complete set and starts proving trials. A programme to refurbish the Class 50s at Doncaster, aimed at improving reliability, commences. Class 50 engines are starting to appear on Waterloo to Exeter services. Deliveries of the Class 508 electric multiple unit, eventually intended for the Merseyrail network, begin on the Southern Region. Six Western Region Class 47s are named and nameplates are reinstated on those named back in the 1960s. Only three Class 24s are at work, plus four each of Class 44 and 84. Finsbury Park depot paints some of its Deltics with white cabs, while a visitor to Doncaster works in January sees eleven of the class there.

The old Glasgow Central Railway, closed in 1964, is re-opened as an electrified route by British Rail with a new station at Argyle Street, between Glasgow Central and Glasgow Cross. The Pemnmanshiel tunnel diversion on the East Coast Main Line is opened. British Rail decides to order a batch of Mark 3 sleeper cars. A new titled train, the 'Hull Executive', is inaugurated. Plans for a new joint Ffestiniog and British Rail station at Blaenau Ffestiniog get the go ahead and it is opened in 1982. A survey shows BR still has 2,000 mechanical signal boxes.

Paddington sees a steam train for the first time since 1965 (Castle No. 7029 *Clun Castle*). On the Ffestiniog Railway, a new and modernised (dare we say ugly?) design of double Fairlie engine, *Earl of Merioneth*, enters service. The first ex-Barry scrapyard rebuilt light Pacific to return to service is No. 34016 *Bodmin* at the Mid-Hants Railway.

1980

The last Class 24 in service, No. 24081, is withdrawn from Crewe. Scrapping of Class 45 starts and the final three Class 44s in service are withdrawn. The first two Deltics, Nos 55001/20, are taken out of service. The last Wirral and Mersey Southport line Class 502 unit, built by the LMS, is retired. The last of the troublesome Class 84 AC electrics are also withdrawn. The BRE-Leyland LEV-1 railbus, basically a Leyland National bus body on a rail chassis, enters service after many months of testing. Class 50 No. 50035 is repainted in the new 'large logo' BR livery. Nos 50035, 56036 and 47170 are the only engines currently in the large logo blue livery.

The freight line from Louth to Grimsby is closed. Bury Bolton Street station closes. Diesel multiple units start an hourly Victoria–Gatwick service.

In May, Rocket 150 commemorates the opening of the Liverpool & Manchester Railway with many historic locomotives present.

1981

No. 20050, the first production BR main-line diesel built following the Modernisation Plan, is withdrawn for preservation as D8000. Class 46 No. 46001 is restored to service from store. The APT-P gathers a reputation for problems despite one run from London to Glasgow that achieves the ambitious schedule of 255 minutes for 401 miles. In December the Class 370 APT trains enter regular service. Also at the end of the year the final Deltic-hauled service train is run, the class having latterly often been seen on trains from Liverpool to York, and their erstwhile home, Finsbury Park diesel depot, closes. The Class 140, a prototype of the later Pacer, is launched and starts trials between Leeds and Ilkley. The last train runs over the Woodhead route with electric traction. The line, long a favourite of enthusiasts, is closed between Hadfield and Penistone, ending its use as a through route.

The tracks are mothballed but will later be lifted. West Yorkshire PTE announces ambitious plans to increase services and re-open stations. However, the Clayton West line and that from Denby Dale to Sheffield are slated for closure, with the latter eventually surviving. Another closure is the route from Northampton to Market Harborough. The Welshpool & Llanfair Light Railway re-opens to Welshpool Raven Square. The Wallingford branch closes. Rail services involving individual wagon loads are coming to an end. More than 300 Mark 1 coaches are withdrawn. Steam working ends at Acton Lane CEGB Power Station in London. The Friends of the Settle–Carlisle Railway organisation is formed. Approval is granted for electrifying the Colchester–Ipswich–Norwich route. West Midlands PTE announces fare rises, some as high as 67 per cent.

A new main-line engine is Somerset and Dorset 2-8-0 No. 53809. Barry scrapyard exits include Nos 7903 *Foremark Hall*, 34007 *Wadebridge* and 2-8-0 No. 48624. Great Central 4-4-0 No. 506 *Butler-Henderson* and the Stirling Single return to service. Meanwhile, appeals are running for Merchant Navy Pacifics, Deltics and various other Barry survivors. Bulleid Pacific No. 34092 *City of Wells* becomes famed for its performance over the Settle–Carlisle line, while Stanier Pacific No. 46229 *Duchess of Hamilton* is returned to steam and is equally revered.

1982

British Rail passenger services are divided into three sectors covering local and commuter trains in the south-east of England (Network SouthEast), long-distance expresses (InterCity) and local trains in the other regions of Britain (Regional Railways). The last Deltics, Nos 55002/9/15/22, are withdrawn at the beginning of the year and all are preserved. Nos 55009 *Alycidon* and 55019 *Royal Highland Fusilier* are bought in working order by the Deltic Preservation Society for £50,000. No. 55016 *Gordon Highlander* is the sixth Deltic to be saved. Suddenly, it seems as though every train you see has a different livery. The last Class 82 and 83 electrics are withdrawn. In December, the new 'modular' designed Class 58 freight locomotive, No. 58001, is revealed in the new yellow, red and grey Railfreight livery. It sets a trend for more new liveries, and is modified three years later into two-tone grey with colourful sector markings. 4-SUB unit No. 4732 has been painted in Southern Railway livery. The York-built Class 455 electric multiple units enter service. Thirteen Class 46 engines are reinstated from store at Swindon for use by Freightliner Ltd. BR orders twenty two-car diesel units of Class 141, based on the Class 140 'Pacer' prototype. Another diesel unit prototype is the Class 210, intended for the Southern Region, but it is never ordered in production form.

The Moorgate to Bedford line is electrified and BR announces a 9.5 per cent fare rise – below inflation! All types of passenger stock are now being repainted in blue and grey – plain blue as a rolling stock livery is finished. The Worsborough branch near Barnsley is lifted. After talks with the Friends of the Settle–Carlisle Railway, BR spends £250,000 on waterproofing the deck of Ribblehead Viaduct. However, overnight parcels trains using the Settle–Carlisle line are being re-routed. Fitzwilliam becomes the first new railway station in West Yorkshire for fifteen years. In an example of creatively using a redundant and oversized station building, the Victorian station at Halifax is converted into an industrial heritage centre. Passenger trains return to Templecombe station. Mark 3 air-conditioned sleeper cars are introduced on the West Coast route. HST units are introduced on the Midland Main Line. A last train is run from Barnstaple to Torrington before the closure of the line. A labour dispute has halted the launch of the Bedford–Moorgate electrified service. It is announced that Shildon and Horwich works are to close and Swindon is to be run down. The year is notable for endless industrial disputes.

The Ffestiniog Railway completes its line back to Blaenau Ffestiniog. A plan is launched to rebuild No. 4942 *Maindy Hall* as a 'Saint' Class locomotive, to be running by 1985. The Midland Railway project at Butterley starts operations. The Romney, Hythe & Dymchurch Railway is facing serious financial issues, with falling passenger numbers and worrying losses. Hastings line diesel electric multiple units Nos 1001 and 1013 are purchased for preservation. 'Merchant Navy' Pacific No. 35027 *Port Line* leaves Barry, having been trapped behind twenty-four other locomotives, and is returned to steam in only five years.

1983

Three Class 25s are converted as train heating units. Big inroads are made into the fleets of Class 25 and 08 due to withdrawals. Also withdrawn are the last Ayrshire Coast Class 126 diesel units and the Swindon InterCity Class 123 units, together with the last Southern 4-SUB electrics. The first Modernisation Plan main line diesel, D8000 (No. 20002), is sent to Doncaster for restoration at the National Railway Museum.

BR formally announces that it wants to close the Settle-Carlisle line. It also says that once the Hunts Cross electrification scheme is complete in Merseyside, the line from Rock Ferry to Hooton will be electrified with third rail. Bedford St Johns station is to close and branch trains from Bletchley are diverted to Bedford Midland, with a new halt serving the north of the town. Loughborough (BR) station is to receive a major facelift. BR says it plans to close London Broad Street station and axes the Clayton West branch in Yorkshire at the beginning of the year. It also plans to convert the Manchester–Glossop/Hadfield line to 25 kV AC working from its present 1,500 DC. The Preston–Lindsey Oil Refinery train, a favourite today with enthusiasts, is reported as running unusually with a Class 56 in charge (today you still get a 56 quite often – some things do not change!) Templecombe station is re-opened on a three-year trial basis, following a very long campaign by residents. It had closed back in 1966.

The Science Museum is to build a working reproduction of the Great Western broad gauge *Iron Duke* locomotive. The new 'Royalty and Railway' exhibition at Windsor features a full scale model of GWR 4-2-2 No. 3041 *The Queen.* The supplement to travel on the 'Scarborough Spa Express' over the normal fare is just £1! The Ffestiniog Railway finally opens its new joint station with BR at Blaenau Ffestiniog, the first regular narrow gauge passenger trains there since 1939. A series of railtours to commemorate the sixtieth birthday of *Flying Scotsman* is sold out with long waiting lists. Robert Riddles, the last steam chief mechanical engineer, dies at the age of ninety-one.

1984

The last Class 46 in service is withdrawn, along with the Class 124 Trans-Pennine units, which are replaced by Class 31-hauled trains. The first Class 150 Sprinter, No. 150001, start its tests and eventually 137 are delivered. Former Class 15 BTH Type 1 D8233, latterly a train heating unit, is purchased for preservation. Class 87 engines in new liveries include No. 87012 *Coeur de Lion* in InterCity colours and No. 87006 *City of Glasgow* in experimental grey. An order for seventy-five new Pacer units is split between BR-Leyland Vehicles and Walter Alexander of Firth.

The Wenford Bridge branch in Cornwall is closed. Test runs of the non-stop 'Gatwick Express' trains using Class 73 electro-diesel locomotives take place prior to a service launch in May. 'The Fenman' titled train runs between Liverpool Street and King's Lynn, a reincarnation of a train that ran in steam days. It operates until 1990. The world's first ticket machine to accept credit cards is tested at Euston station. The cars of the 'Manchester Pullman' are all named. BR states that eighteen stations will lose their freight service. Auchinleck and Kilmaurs stations are re-opened in Scotland, together with Saltaire in West Yorkshire. Unions at Swindon works are warned that the plant will close unless new orders are won. The Class 506 1,500 V DC electric multiple units are withdrawn following conversion of the Manchester–Glossop line to AC working. A magnetic levitation train starts operating between Birmingham International station and Birmingham Airport. Extra trains are run on the Settle–Carlisle line, but BR still insists it wants to close the route. BR also gives notice that it wants to shut stations served by the line's Dalesrail weekend service, popular with hikers.

A series of steam trips between Fort William and Mallaig is planned for the summer. The Llangollen Railway is granted a Light Railway Order from Llangollen to Carrog. The Gloucestershire Warwickshire Railway runs its first passenger train.

1985

The last three Class 40s are withdrawn in January leaving just celebrity engine D200 in service. In March, the old Class 503 units, some dating back to 1938, are finally displaced on Merseyrail by 508s from the Southern Region, but one unit is restored to LMS livery to work from Liverpool to Hooton. No. 27007 becomes the first Class 27 to be saved for preservation. BR has orders for sixty-nine Pacers, 228 second generation diesel multiple units and forty-six electric multiple units in a rush to eliminate older trains with blue asbestos by the end of 1987. The influx of Sprinters and Pacers condemns many first generation diesel multiple units to the scrapyard. For the 150th anniversary of the Great Western, five diesels, Nos 47079, 47484, 47628, 47500 and 50007, are painted green and named. With the end of hump-shunting at Tinsley, the last Class 13, No. 13003, is withdrawn and sent to Doncaster for scrap. The prototype HST power car, No. 41001, is prepared for display at York Railway Museum. Class 83 No. 83009 is reinstated for Euston–Willesden empty stock working, alongside Nos 82005, 82008, 83012 and 83015. Warship No. D818 *Glory* is scrapped thirteen years after being withdrawn; it had been kept at Swindon. A decline in coal traffic signals the end of many older locomotives. The APT-P experiment, unloved, under-funded and damned by an anti-railway media, is over and most units are quietly scrapped. Much of its groundbreaking technology went on to be used in other trains.

It is announced that the Calder Valley main line will be the main Trans-Pennine freight route, but the line's stations become unstaffed halts. Red Star becomes the market leader in parcel deliveries. A new depot at Rochdale will provide BR with 300 miles of continuous-welded rail each year. New liveries abound, from Express Parcels to Cornish Railways – all of a sudden the railways are colourful again. West Yorkshire PTE proposes closing Altofts and Woodlesford station, but only the former is eventually shut. The experimental Class 151 Metro-Cammell unit is operating on the Matlock branch. The 'Master Cutler' express makes its last run as a titled train after thirty-eight years. Authorisation is given by the Conservative government – seen as rather anti-rail – for the electrification of the East Coast route.

1986

The final Class 86/2 to be named is No. 86238 *European Community*. The first Class 318 unit for the Glasgow–Ayr route is delivered. The first Class 47 withdrawals, apart from accidents, commence. They are the non-standard pilot engines from the 47401–20 batch. Class 45s hand over the Liverpool–Newcastle service to Class 47s. The Hastings line diesel electric multiple units are retired when the route is electrified. The first privately owned Class 59 enters service, along with the first Class 150/1 Sprinters. BR also orders twenty Class 87/2 electrics, eventually delivered as Class 90. Pacers – called Skippers in the South West – start work in Devon and Cornwall.

Network SouthEast sector is launched to replace previous regional areas and provide services to London and the surrounding area. The bright new livery is red, white, blue and grey. The short-lived London & South East Sector Express livery – a strange brown and fawn with an orange stripe – is introduced. ScotRail, another new sector, uses InterCity livery with a blue rather than red stripe. The first PORTIS (a portable ticket-issuing machine) is introduced on the Watford–St Albans Abbey line. A rail link from Liverpool Street to Stansted Airport gets the go ahead. Work starts on building a new Salford Crescent station. In Manchester the Hazel Grove chord opens, linking the Buxton and New Mills Central lines. Barmouth Bridge on the Cambrian line re-opens after £1.8 million is spent clearing molluscs. It is announced that 5,000 jobs will be lost in BR workshops, mainly at Doncaster and Wolverton. BR introduces the slogan 'We're Getting There'. London's Broad Street station closes.

A major return to service is 4-6-2 No. 4468 *Mallard,* while No. 71000 *Duke of Gloucester* moves in steam for the first time since 1962.

1987

The last Class 25 engines are withdrawn in March. Mass withdrawals of Class 27 render the class extinct, with their being outlived by the older Class 26. The ungainly Class 89 No. 89001, designed by Brush to a BR specification, carries out successful trials and the first Class 90 is delivered. No. 50011 *Centurion* is the first Class 50 to be withdrawn, with others following. With the Class 50s facing an uncertain future, No. 50049 *Defiance* is modified as a freight locomotive and renumbered

50149, but the project is not a success. Many Class 45s are in store at March depot. Hasting diesel unit No. 203001 is outshopped in green livery. HST power car No. 43167 arrives at Derby works to have its Paxman Valenta engine replaced by a new Mirrlees unit. Deliveries of the fifty Class 58 freight locomotives are completed, but hoped for export sales fail to materialise. Class 144 Pacers enter service in West Yorkshire. Five withdrawn London Transport Tube trains from 1938 are restored to service. York deliver Sprinters of Class 150/2 for Trans-Pennine local services and the first new Class 155/3 Sprinters are delivered, initially for the Cardiff area. No. 33008, named *Eastleigh*, is repainted into its original green livery, and Class 86/2 locomotives start work between Liverpool Street, Cambridge and Norwich. InterCity fares rise by 10 per cent. The final Class 37/5 is delivered. After Pacers prove unsuitable due to overcrowding and problems on sharp curves, veteran Class 108s replace them on the Gunnislake branch in Cornwall. Heysham, closed since 1975, is re-opened. The Coventry–Nuneaton line is also re-opened to passengers after twenty-two years, along with the Kettering to Corby route; but the battle to save the Settle–Carlisle line rages on. A new Birmingham Snow Hill station opens providing, at first, local services, but eventually a new link to London Marylebone using a revived Chiltern main line. Electrified services commence at the southern end of the East Coast Main Line.

By 1987 BR has lost control of its corporate image to the extent that a whole series of unrelated liveries are in use. These included many engines still in plain blue, some in 'large logo' blue, InterCity red stripe and a variation known as Main Line, ScotRail, plus various freight colours. Both old and newer Railfreight grey can be seen, plus a three-grey sector livery and a whole raft of minor liveries such as British Steel blue and dark green with a white roof applied to certain Class 20s. It seems as though anything goes, the only common factor – in *most* cases – being the use of the double arrow symbol.

M7 0-4-4 tank No. 30053 is brought home from the USA. The nameplate from Jubilee 4-6-0 No. 45742 *Connaught* is sold for £550. The Keighley and Worth Valley Railway rebuilds the old Foulbridge station buildings brick by brick at its Ingrow West location.

1988

Class 442 electric multiple units are delivered for the Bournemouth and Weymouth line, replacing the 4-REP units. This coincides with the start of electrified services between Bournemouth and Weymouth, replacing diesel-hauled trains. D200 (No. 40122), after nearly five years back at work, is retired to the National Railway Museum. Meanwhile, sister locomotives Nos 40012 *Aureol*, 40013 *Andania*, 40118 and 40135 are saved for preservation. BR confirms it will not rescind its ban on allowing preserved diesels on the main lines. Nos 31106 and 33114 become the last of their class to receive heavy general overhauls, at Doncaster and Eastleigh respectively. The first Class 37, No. 37350, is repainted green and also carries its former number, D6700. Brush is contracted to build 100 Class 60 freight engines. Veteran electric No. 83009 is now the last of the Class 82 and 83 locomotives at work, all others having been withdrawn and stored. No. 89001 *Avocet* starts work. Class 31s are retired from Trans-Pennine express services in favour of diesel multiple units. Class 47/7 No. 47713 *Tayside Region* is the first of its class to be withdrawn, due to fire damage. The last 03 shunter is withdrawn from Ipswich. All remaining 'Peaks' except No. 45106 are withdrawn. The first Class 321 is unveiled.

Preserved EM2 No. 27000 *Electra* is restored in green livery. Class 90 and 91 electrics are being delivered simultaneously, but few of the former are actually at work. Pacer No. 141109 becomes the first of its class to appear in West Yorkshire PTA maroon livery. The same PTA takes delivery of seven Class 155 units (they are still working on West Yorkshire lines in 2018).

Private companies are invited to bid for the Settle–Carlisle railway, which the government says has no future other than as a tourist railway, and for which use BR is not 'well qualified'. The Skegness line becomes an enthusiast favourite thanks to its semaphore signals, level crossings and a general lack of modernisation. The link between Lichfield City and Trent Valley stations is re-opened to passenger trains. Two other routes re-opening to passengers are Walsall to Hednesford and Abercynon to Aberdare, both freight only. The Watford to St Albans Abbey branch is electrified. The National Union of Railwaymen refuses to allow a Class 59 to be used on a railtour on the grounds that it is imported. The last train runs from Oakamoor Sand Sidings. BR Engineering Ltd (BREL) is privatised. Barry scrapyard has just a handful of engines left. ScotRail bans smoking in first class. Bedworth station re-opens near Nuneaton. Thameslink services start.

An LMS Class 8F 2-8-0, formerly No. 8274, is purchased in Turkey and returned to the UK. *Flying Scotsman* is drawing the crowds on a visit to Australia. BR's last steam train runs on the Vale of Rheidol Railway on 18 December prior to its takeover by preservationists.

1989

The last Class 45 in service, No. 45106, repainted green in 1988 for special working, is withdrawn and scrapped after catching fire. The former D8243, the last surviving Class 15 converted to a pre-heating unit, is withdrawn and scrapped. Built in 1938 as Tube trains for London, the first of nine Class 483 units are delivered to the Isle of Wight. Class 86 No. 86401 becomes Network SouthEast's only AC electric locomotive and is named *Northampton Town*. Class 156 Sprinters take over services on the West Highland line and are still there nearly thirty years later. The East Coast Main Line between London, Doncaster and Leeds is electrified. 'King' Class locomotive No. 6024 *King Edward I* returns to steam. The last 03 shunter on the mainland, No. 03170, is withdrawn, leaving two on the Isle of Wight. Class 321 electric multiple units are delivered for Network SouthEast services from Euston and Liverpool Street. Two Hastings line diesel units are secured for preservation. The first driving van trailer (DVT) for the West Coast route, No. 82101, is delivered. A number of organisations are seeking to preserve all or part of the Wymondham–North Elham line in Norfolk. Oxford station is being rebuilt. Four PTEs are seeking compensation from BR for the poor reliability and performance of Pacer Class 141, 142, 143 and 144 units they are using. BR announces that its standard locomotive liveries will be InterCity, Mainline, Railfreight (with sector markings) and General, a grey colour scheme. The route of the high-speed rail link to the Channel Tunnel is announced. Three serious rail accidents take place within a few days. Sheffield Victoria station, closed since 1970, is finally demolished.

1990

In September, the first of a new diesel multiple unit called Express Sprinter (Class 158) is delivered from Derby works for longer distance cross-country routes. Work on building new platforms at Waterloo for international services through the Channel Tunnel commences. The last two surviving Class 25 ETHEL heating units are withdrawn. An organisation has been created with the intention of building a new A1 Pacific. Work on installing the infrastructure for a Metro system is taking place at Manchester Victoria. The unique Class 47/9 diesel, with a Class 58 engine, is withdrawn. David Mitchell, Transport Minister, says that if no bidders come forward the Settle–Carlisle line will close. GWR 4575 Class tank No. 5553 becomes the last steam engine to leave Woodham Brothers at Barry in January 1990 for the West Somerset Railway, twenty-two years after the first departure. Ten other unsold engines stay at Barry, but most are eventually dispersed. Meanwhile, No. 34072 *257 Squadron*, purchased from Barry in 1984, is returned to steam after a restoration taking just two years.

We start our photographic survey on a misty morning in March 1976 with a new HST set racing towards Reading. The new strategy for British Rail's diesel express trains is in place. (Bob Mullins)

Here we have a type of locomotive that had no future on BR. A scruffy Class 52, No. 1068 *Western Reliance*, has been reduced to hauling empty mineral wagons through Reading in January 1976. (Bob Mullins)

This picture was taken on 19 December 1976 and shows Class 87 No. 87005 rushing a northbound express through Barby, Northamptonshire. The north portal of Kilsby Tunnel is in the distance while the line of trees to the far left marks the Rugby–Northampton line.

Racing through Sandy in the mist in early 1977 with a northbound express is a Deltic. The signal box, sidings and man walking along the track seem to perfectly capture a railway that was to rapidly disappear. (Bob Mullins)

In January 1977 the last 'Western' diesel to be given an overhaul clung to life. Here, No. 1023 *Western Fusilier* is at Moreton-in-Marsh on a railtour with an unsightly headboard. The following month the 'Western' saga was over for British Rail and No. 1023 was claimed for the national collection. (Bob Mullins)

Sharnbrook, on the Midland Main Line between Bedford and Wellingborough, offers freight trains a gentler climb than passenger services, as seen here with a Class 47 on tanks in March 1977. Ten years after this picture, the freight lines were singled – unimaginable in the 1960s when a steady stream of freight trains occupied the lines. (Bob Mullins)

A scene that has been eliminated from our railways – a Class 08 shunter at Wigston South Junction with a mixed transfer freight. This engine reversed its trip freight into the yard on the right on 17 September 1978.

A Brush Class 31 heads north along the Midland Main Line with a very mixed freight. Wigston South Junction, 17 September 1978.

Winding its way alongside the inlet at Weymouth is a boat train headed by Class 33/1 No. 33113 in August 1978. The white hatching marks areas where you must not park. You can see a nice selection of classic cars and boats.

In October 1978, the light is fading fast as Brush Class 31 No. 31217 arrives at King's Cross with a rake of Travelling Post Office vans to form a mail train. A familiar sight for many years, the TPOs disappeared in 2004.

Obviously this is Derby station and reversing through is Class 45/1 No. 45137 *The Bedfordshire and Hertfordshire Regiment TA*. The date is 24 July 1979 and I seem to recall the station was heaving with traffic during my twenty minutes' stop to change trains.

On 15 August 1979, the overhead power was off at Birmingham New Street station. Class 40 No. 40025 *Lusitania* has arrived hauling Class 86 No. 86250. Meanwhile, Class 47 No. 47252 is pulling into the adjacent platform, also with an electric in tow, this time No. 87005 *City of London*. The coupling between *Lusitania* and the Class 86 seems to be the centre of attention.

Many people will recognise this as Radcliffe-on-Soar power station and here we have a train of Presflo wagons containing fly ash leaving the site and heading south on the Midland Main Line. The engine is a new Class 56 (delivered about six weeks earlier) No. 56058, earning its keep on 9 August 1979 and the billowing steam from the cooling towers gives a bit of atmosphere.

Having been replaced by HST units on the East Coast Main Line, the Deltics could be found on a variety of workings that took them well off their old stamping ground. Here, No. 55022 *Royal Scots Grey* is seen at Carlisle in August 1979. (Bob Mullins)

A merry-go-round freight heads through Burton-on-Trent station on 16 August 1979. In charge is Class 56 No. 56044. This engine was still quite new, having been built at Doncaster the previous year. The Double Diamond brewery is receiving some refurbishment.

These engines are passing Hemington in Derbyshire on 25 September 1979 with an eastbound coal train (and an incorrect headcode). It seemed that all over Derbyshire you could come across a railway line and a few minutes later a pair of these old English Electric engines would busily pass with a train of coal wagons.

It's five o'clock on 18 September 1979 and here is an everyday occurrence. The Birmingham RCW three-car diesel unit bound for Nottingham is arriving under the delicate canopies of Loughborough (Midland) station and everyone is getting ready to board. A nice display of hanging baskets shows pride in the station at a time when this was not always the case.

These engines were built by Metropolitan-Vickers and not long after this picture was taken they started going into store. But here, No. 82003 is still giving good service, hustling a short freight complete with guard's van to Birmingham on the Rugby to Birmingham line through Hampton-in-Arden station on 29 August 1979. Built in 1960, she was withdrawn in 1983.

This was a day when I simply could not persuade the authorities to let me go round the shed at Toton. Instead I had to content myself with this general view. Engines visible include Nos 20209, 20003, 20047, 47229, and Peak No. 44007 *Ingleborough*. This was 9 August 1979 and it was my last ever attempt to sweet-talk my way around a BR shed.

A view of Smethwick in Birmingham, where the canal and the railway run side by side. The train is heading away from the camera towards Wolverhampton and comprises Class 310 unit No. 310054 on 24 August 1979, still in plain blue. Later they were repainted blue and grey. Soho Train Maintenance Depot is in the distance. The wake from the narrow boat is bouncing off the banks.

Here's an unlikely pairing at Stoke-on-Trent station on 5 October 1979. On the left is Class 44 No. 44008 *Penyghent* with a freight for the Derby line; in the platform, and taking precedence, is Class 87 No. 87034 *William Shakespeare* on its way to London Euston from Manchester Piccadilly.

Back in the late 1970s I heard that trains were still using the Great Central north of Loughborough from time to time. On this occasion I got lucky and this train came past with a very unusual load of military-owned vehicles for auction at Ruddington. Here, on 1 October 1979, we see Class 47 No. 47340 near Stanford, looking towards Loughborough.

This is Melton Mowbray Town station, also on 1 October 1979. A pair of Class 20 diesels, Nos 20063 and 20190, head west on a perfect evening with a fairly long freight comprising coal empties. Compared with my previous visit here in 1972, the huge bracket signal at the end of the platform has gone, as have the signals guarding the left-hand line.

To mark the centenary of train catering, a selection of catering vehicles from Travellers' Fare and the National Railway Museum was taken around the country behind (I seem to recall) No. 6000 *King George V.* Here we see the train on display at Birmingham Moor Street on 20 September 1979.

On 1 November 1979, Class 47 diesel No. 47027 heads south with piped empties along the Midland Main Line as storm clouds approach. The chimneys are those of the Brush works at Loughborough. In the distance is the Great Central overbridge, now being rebuilt, and Loughborough Midland station; behind the train is a spur to the Great Central.

Beautifully prepared, Deltic No. 55013 *The Black Watch* is seen at Doncaster in February 1980. (Bob Mullins)

Reddish was the depot for the Class 76 locomotives that hauled freights across the Woodhead route. By 29 June 1980, when this pair was photographed, the writing was on the wall for the railway and it closed the following year. The locomotives are Nos 76038 and 76035. (Gordon Edgar)

A coal train passes through Newport on 14 February 1981. The unusual combination of motive power has brought Class 37 No. 37293 and Class 56 No. 56035 together. (Gordon Edgar).

The Class 46 version of the 'Peak' diesels had a long association with the west of England on both passenger and freight duties. One of their regular turns was clay hoods between Cornwall and the Stoke area, and here No. 46009 is on just such a working at Par in March 1981. (Bob Mullins)

Casualties in the 1980s included many smaller shunters that made life more interesting. Andrew Barclay Class 06 0-4-0 diesel mechanical shunter No. 06003 was transferred from Scotland to Reading to act as the yard shunter at the Signal & Telegraph works, being allocated departmental number 97804. It was made redundant and preserved when the works closed in 1984. It is seen here at Reading depot on 27 April 1981. (Gordon Edgar)

This is a fair load for a Class 25 – No. 25183 is seen clambering slowly up the Lickey Incline on 17 July 1981.

With the Deltics facing extinction, a number of railtours took them off the beaten track. Here, No. 55007 *Pinza* is seen at Finsbury Park depot on 12 September 1981 with a red buffer beam, ready to visit Ipswich and Spalding with the 'Deltic Anglian'. She was withdrawn for scrap three months later. (Bob Mullins)

At Barnt Green in heavy snow, a Derby six-car train for New Street pauses under the elegant Midland footbridge on 3 January 1982. Note the white car with a blue stripe – another short-lived attempt to update the blue livery.

There are days when you should stay at home, but for some reason I clambered out of bed on 5 January 1982, and before struggling to work I wandered across to nearby Barnt Green station as a blizzard was in force. Here we see a southbound train hurrying through the station on a day when road traffic was paralysed. The tracks in the foreground lead to Redditch.

On 21 January 1982 the sun came out after morning snow. I am at Kings Norton, in the southern outskirts of Birmingham, to watch a Class 47 passing on a southbound train, but a flurry of snow as the engine passed meant I could not get the number. This platform has long been abandoned.

This was a great day out on the 'Cumbrian Mountain Pullman', featuring two LMS engines, Class 5 4-6-0 No. 5407 and the Pacific *Duchess of Hamilton*. Each of the engines did run-pasts at stations. The trip was on 20 February 1982 and this view is at Wennington.

On 9 February 1982, Class 45 No. 45059 *Royal Engineer* arrives at snowy Newcastle with a parcels train.

This was a bitterly cold day at Newcastle station, with my finger almost freezing on my Pentax camera. Class 40 No. 40192 got my attention as it ran through the station light engine on 22 February 1982.

A contrast in front ends at Scarborough station on 8 August 1982: Class 45/1 No. 45114 waits to leave with an excursion, while I am waiting to return to Leeds behind West Country Class 4-6-2 No. 34092 *City of Wells*.

The last passenger train of the day heads north at Ribblehead Viaduct on 20 April 1983, with a Class 47 hauling just four coaches. The Settle–Carlisle line clings to life, but BR sees no future for it.

On 27 April 1983 a Class 50 diesel heads out of Leamington Spa. The engine is No. 50034 *Furious* in large logo livery. These engines were a common sight here at the time, working from Paddington to Birmingham New Street through Leamington Spa and Coventry.

A three-car Class 116 diesel multiple unit rumbles past allotments at Warwick on 17 May 1983. These units will be remembered for their lively ride and weak structure, which meant the doors were sometimes difficult to shut with a full load.

This is Claverdon station in Warwickshire, served by trains on the Leamington Spa to Stratford route. The station was built in the late 1930s with double track, but in 1969 the line here was singled. A Derby diesel multiple unit approaches the platform on the evening of 14 May 1983.

At Leamington Spa station on 6 June 1983, Class 121 diesel railcar W55006 is seen leaving the rather weedy tracks on its way to Stratford-upon-Avon, with other diesel multiple units in the background. A Class 47 waits to leave for London. This picture has a kind of sterility due to the absence of people, but dare I say I quite like it?

A general view of Manchester Victoria station on 13 June 1983, with various diesel multiple units and a smart Class 08 shunter in the platforms. Note the amazing weeds. These are the bays at the east end and you can just see a Calder Valley DMU among the stock with a Bury EMU on the far left.

This is Cross Gates station, Leeds, on 15 June 1983. Heading uphill is one of those neat Trans-Pennine four-car diesel multiple units of Class 124, which looked very swish when they were introduced.

On 15 June 1983 the first Class 33 locomotive, No. 33001, is seen at Crewe departing for the south with a passenger train heading to Cardiff. It clearly has some rail fans in the first coach.

Ex-works Class 37 No. 37051 stands at Darlington on 9 February 1983. It is matched to the Doncaster works test train and is waiting for a path southwards. After forty-five years of service, it was scrapped in 2008.

Passing the loops at Blea Moor is a Brush Class 31 locomotive with the afternoon train from Carlisle to Leeds on 21 June 1983. Blea Moor Tunnel is in the background, while the signal box, stone walls and cottages are typical features of the line. Whernside is on the left.

Smokey Class 47 No. 47501 crosses Ribblehead Viaduct, on 21 June 1983. These trains were much more interesting than the Class 158 multiple units used today, but the service was at its lowest ebb, with most intermediate stations having been closed.

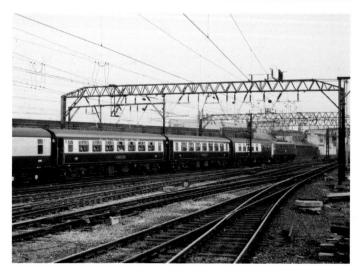

The Metro-Cammell Pullman cars indicate this is a special train. In fact, No. 85035 is leaving Crewe on 22 June 1983 with the 'Cumbrian Mountain Pullman' stock. The cars of this Mark 1 design were built in 1960 and 1961 for the East Coast route; later, some were used on ordinary trains between Liverpool Street and Norwich.

Here we have a Class 86/3 locomotive at Manchester Piccadilly station on 22 June 1983. These were basically Class 86/0 engines fitted with improved wheels. It later became No. 86426 and was withdrawn in June 2004. This is my only picture (among more than eighty of Class 86) of an 86/3.

A parcels train is loaded at Manchester Piccadilly station on 22 June 1983. In charge is one of the dwindling fleet of Class 40 diesels, No. 40099. About sixty of these engines were still at work at this time. The headcode discs have been removed.

These Swindon cross-country units were common on the services from Birmingham to Peterborough and beyond in the 1970s and 1980s. Here we see one (set No. 522) arriving at Hinckley station with a westbound service on 7 July 1983. By the end of the 1980s, all had been withdrawn.

Plenty of action at Doncaster on 18 August 1983. A locally built Class 56, No. 56073, heads through the station with southbound merry-go-round empties, while another Class 56 is seen passing through the platform and an HST waits to head north.

A Leeds to Morecambe DMU comprising a Metro-Cammell unit runs through Gargrave on 21 June 1983. Passengers had a great view out of the cab windows in many older multiple units.

Class 25/2 No. 25202 from Carlisle Kingmoor depot is seen here rumbling through Huddersfield's grand station on 18 August 1983 with a bulk train of coke empties from Holyhead to Humber Oil Refinery. A Calder Valley DMU of Class 110 waits at the platform. Both of these types had only a few years of life remaining.

Another Class 40 and another parcels train. This one is seen passing through Sheffield Midland station on 8 August 1983 behind Class 40 diesel No. 40029 *Saxonia*.

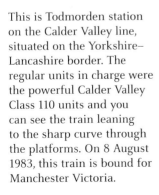

This is Todmorden station on the Calder Valley line, situated on the Yorkshire–Lancashire border. The regular units in charge were the powerful Calder Valley Class 110 units and you can see the train leaning to the sharp curve through the platforms. On 8 August 1983, this train is bound for Manchester Victoria.

On 9 August 1983, the magnificent Pacific No. 46229 *Duchess of Hamilton* stands at York station before giving us a good run to Scarborough. The oversized smokebox number plate was fitted at Swindon during its restoration, later being replaced by one with correctly sized numbers. Sadly, we probably won't see her running again.

My travels round Yorkshire in August 1983 have now taken me to Ilkley station on this Metro-Cammell DMU, when it was one of the last gas-lit stations in the UK. This is a station that has since changed completely, with services now electrified and the buildings you see here converted into a supermarket and shops.

Maybe you can recall Bradford Forster Square station in steam days. This sad picture, taken on 17 August 1983, shows how it had descended into near oblivion from a huge and important station. It's hard to imagine the expresses that called here in its halcyon years. These are the spacious passenger platforms – the goods depot was to the left.

Looking east at Brough station, in Yorkshire, on 18 August 1983. At this time there were two extra through tracks outside the platforms. The station was served by Trans-Pennine and King's Cross–Hull trains, such as this HST with the driver wearing the Gendarme-style hat. The buildings shown here have since been swept away and replaced by quite decent new ones.

Goole station on 10 August 1983 and standing in the platform with a train for Leeds is a Derby Class 114 twin unit. There is some very interesting-looking industrial archaeology in the background. I wonder if it still exists today. Visiting all these stations, many of them built by the North Eastern Railway, was a very enjoyable experience.

Arriving at Leeds station in a downpour on 9 August 1983 is Brush Type 2 No. 31108, which had started life as D5526, hence its lack of a headcode panel. It must have been a shocking summer that year.

This shot depicts Selby station and its swing bridge. Running light through the station on 10 August 1983 is one of the ubiquitous Class 47 engines, No. 47518, from Gateshead. It hardly looks like the East Coast Main Line. Passengers are about to cross the railway under the supervision of a station staff member, as the footbridge was unsuitable for people with mobility issues.

On this day I took a ride behind D200 on the Settle–Carlisle line. Here she is at Keighley station where I commenced my journey on 9 August 1983 on the 16.00 Leeds–Carlisle service, her regular working at the time. This station has changed dramatically over the years, with the university now looming over it. In the 1980s it was weedy and decrepit.

Another Class 47, this time No. 47511 *Thames*, at York station on 11 August 1983. She soon became No. 47714 *Grampian Region* and moved to Scotland. She was one of the later Class 47s, and had been delivered new as D1955 at the end of 1966.

Approaching Hull station in the rain on 16 August 1983 is a Class 123 diesel multiple unit. These were built at Swindon in 1963 and found their way north on Trans-Pennine services after being displaced from more southerly territories. They were all withdrawn the following year and none survived. The shunter is No. 08927.

On 15 June 1983, Class 45 No. 45112 *Royal Army Ordnance Corps* enters Wakefield Westgate station with a short train heading north.

Liverpool Street to Shenfield Class 306 electric multiple units Nos 063 and 038 are seen here in store at Bradford Forster Square on 17 August 1983. They were dumped here for more than a year before being towed to a scrapyard – Cashmore's at Great Bridge, I believe. They added to the desolation at this famous old Midland Railway station.

A train of oxygen tanks from North Wembley's Ditton BOC depot in the evening sunshine at Nuneaton on 17 August 1984, with Class 81 No. 81012 in charge. The huge LNWR goods shed was later demolished and, as so often happened, became the site of a car park. The late 1980s saw the Class 81s gradually withdrawn.

You may remember that, in 1984, BR was experimenting with new liveries to replace the dreary Rail blue. At that time, No. 87006 *City of Glasgow* was repainted in a large logo dark grey livery with red buffer beams, and here we see her waiting to leave Euston on 20 July 1984. Happily this was not a chosen livery, although a lighter grey did become the Railfreight colour.

At Nuneaton station on 17 August 1984, the express speeding through the station northbound, No. 370007, was one of the tilting train units that caused so much controversy at the time. These highly advanced units perished through some bad publicity, but some of the technology went on to be used elsewhere with great success.

Changes are afoot on the Wirral line in 1984. On 25 April that year we see a newly delivered (from the Southern Region) Class 508, still bearing the destination of its last journey, to Effingham Junction in Surrey. An old Class 503 unit stands in the platform at Birkenhead North on its way to Liverpool Central. Before long the 507 and 508 units will be running all services on the Wirral and Mersey lines.

Sometimes an old blue engine and ubiquitous blue and grey stock can produce a very attractive picture, as here with Class 33 No. 33052 *Ashford* at Hereford on 30 March 1984. It is hauling a Crewe–Cardiff service, which was a regular duty for these engines at the time. (Gordon Edgar)

A meeting of trains at Bidston station on the Wirral. Here we are looking west and a Class 503 electric multiple unit (M29134M) is on the left, heading under the M53 motorway towards West Kirby. Recently arrived from Wrexham is a Pressed Steel diesel multiple unit, a service that terminates here. The Wrexham branch curves off to the left. 25 April 1984.

On 3 May 1984, a diesel multiple unit is seen crossing the Forth Bridge in misty weather. The trains might change, but the Forth Bridge retains its splendour, whether from below or on board a train crossing it.

Seen at Hampton-in-Arden on May 4 1984 is Class 310 No. 310083, operating between Birmingham New Street and Coventry. These units gave thirty-five years of excellent service and the Euston–Birmingham line never seemed the same without them.

In the mid-1980s Waterloo was a sea of blue and grey. The new order is represented by Class 455 No. 5859, which is seen in August 1985 with a service for Dorking. It is still in action today.

The old order – Waterloo station seems strangely peaceful as one of the 2-HAP suburban units waits to leave in July 1985. These 1950s units were being withdrawn at the time.

Marylebone station looks like a building site in August 1985, with just three Derby-built units in the station. It all looks very depressing. Melbury House is in the background, then used by BR and British Waterways.

The AM4 electric multiple units gave more than thirty years' service, latterly running as three-car units. Here, No. 304020 is seen heading south at Atherton's handsome station in September 1985.

Overshadowed by later electric engines, the Class 85s still appeared on top link working in the 1980s. No. 85030 races south through Nuneaton with an express headed by two baggage vans on 30 April 1985.

Waiting to leave Euston in August 1985 with a northbound express is No. 87021 *Robert the Bruce.*

At Birmingham International on 8 January 1985 is No. 50045 *Achilles*, seen at a time when these engines were regular performers on this line. Somehow they didn't seem to stay anywhere for all that long.

Newly repainted in the new Railfreight grey livery is this Class 47 diesel, No. 47366 *The Institute of Civil Engineers*. She is at Nuneaton, waiting to cross from the Up to the Down side in June 1985.

Waiting to leave Tywyn Wharf station on 26 August 1985 is Talyllyn Railway 0-4-2T No. 4 *Edward Thomas*. This picture has a strange vintage feel to it, as though it could have been taken in the 1950s. While everything else was changing, the Talyllyn was reassuringly obdurate.

An image of the brief
transitional period at the
former North London
Railway London Broad
Street station when some
of the Southern Region
2-EPBs were taking over
from the London District
Class 501 units. Here, 2-EPB
No. 6318 stands alongside
No. 501164 on May Day,
1985. The station was closed
on 30 June 1986 and was
used for the Broadgate office
development. (Gordon Edgar)

A Class 50,
No. 50008 *Thunderer,* slowly
leaving Waterloo in
August 1985. This type of
engine could be seen in
four different liveries in
the 1980s, illustrating the
confusing state of BR's
corporate image at the time.

All change in Scotland.
Hybrid Class 107/104 diesel
multiple unit No. 107438 and
Class 107 unit No. 107437
at Ayr station on 23 March
1986, shortly before the
overhead electrification was
switched on. (Gordon Edgar)

Eastfield's Class 27 No. 27053 is seen acting as Glasgow Queen Street station pilot on 24 March 1986. The Class 27 was withdrawn the following year after twenty-five years in service. This is the old North British station and it is still very busy today. (Gordon Edgar)

Coal empties are moving briskly through Cardiff Central station in June 1986 headed by a pair of locally based Class 37s, Nos 37505 and 37501. This line saw huge amounts of coal traffic in the old days. These engines were among the most effective workhorses purchased by BR, quite a few achieving fifty years in service.

One of my favourite 'Merchant Navy' Pacifics is seen here having fallen upon very hard times. The huge challenge of rebuilding a big Pacific means that only five of the ten rescued from Barry scrapyard have been restored. In June 1986, No. 35011 *General Steam Navigation* was near the end of a twenty-year stay at Barry when seen with 2-6-2T No. 4115 alongside. Four years later the Barry saga was over.

The Gatwick Express was an early attempt to provide a fast, intensive specialised service. In June 1986, two years after the launch, I was at Victoria to watch this service depart around lunchtime with Class 73/2 electro-diesel No. 73208 *Croydon 1883–1983*. A sister locomotive, No. 73201, stands alongside.

In August 1986 a long rake of empty hoppers headed by a Railfreight Class 47 takes the Leicester line at Nuneaton. This was BR's freight at its low point; from the 1990s onwards, freight traffic started to rise again after more than thirty years of decline.

The Class 25s were on their last legs in the mid-1980s, but here No. 25034 heads a long train of bogie bolster wagons through Nuneaton in June 1986. Nine months later the class was extinct on British Rail.

A very good friend from Northamptonshire's ironstone railways, 0-6-0ST *Lamport No. 3* is seen in her afterlife. Happily, when her quarry days were over at Lamport, she moved not too far away, firstly to the Great Central and then for service on the Market Bosworth Railway, now the Battlefield Line. She is seen being serviced there on a Sunday in April 1986.

Surrounded by cast-iron supports and old mineral wagons is Class 45/1 No. 45149, which has just arrived at Nuneaton with the evening passenger train from Leicester. This is in June 1986 and the engine has very smart paintwork. Just over a year later she was withdrawn, but luckily survived into preservation.

Birkenhead shunter No. 03170 was spruced up for the open day on 6 April 1986. This type was the last mechanical shunter to survive, but apart from two on the Isle of Wight, all had disappeared by the end of the decade.

On this day I took my tripod and Pentax to Nuneaton station to try a few night shots in the snow. Here we have Class 87 No. 87015 *Howard of Effingham* ready to leave for the north on 12 January 1986.

Seen at Victoria station, London, in June 1986 is this Network South-East Class 455/8 EMU, No. 5834. Its design and livery are in sharp contrast to the Southern Railway and early BR units they replaced. They were built between 1982 and 1984 at York and are still in service.

At Birmingham International in January 1986, this Class 310 unit has been rebuilt without wrap-around windows and was painted in Network SouthEast colours. No. 067 also appeared in the first volume of this series when brand new. The new windows are to protect the driver from hooligans throwing stones at the train.

Looking east at Hebden Bridge station on 2 September 1986. This is a very attractive station, retaining much of its heritage feel, and quite how it survived when so many others were ruined is baffling.

In sharp contrast to Hebden Bridge, this is the next station east on the Calder Valley line, Mytholmroyd, at what must have been its lowest ebb. Now it is safe, busy and carefully tended, with lovely flower beds. This pictures dates from 2 September 1986.

A very lucky shot on 6 April 1986: just outside Hoylake station, the old Wirral line Class 502 unit on a special working passes its successor, Class 508 No. 508113. I had my 135 mm telephoto lens installed and managed this picture with my trusty Pentax ME Super.

A sight to depress any railway enthusiast in April 1986. The train is one of the prototype Metro-Cammel three-car Class 151 units that were in service from 1985 to 1989. It is entering Cromford, once a busy station on the Midland Main Line to Manchester, but here an unloved halt. Its rescue from demolition was probably due to being Grade II listed. After various ambitious plans, the two 151 units were scrapped in 2004, but Cromford is now much improved.

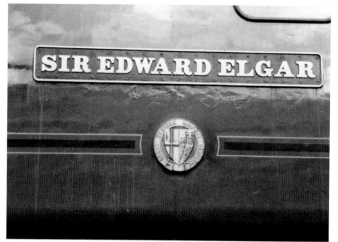

One of the engines repainted to celebrate 150 years of the Great Western Railway in 1984 was Class 50 No. 50007, which also lost its name *Hercules* in favour of *Sir Edward Elgar*. This name had once been carried by 'Castle' Class 4-6-0 No. 7005 and the Class 50 received brass number plates and a representation of Great Western livery, eventually being preserved. It is seen here at Birkenhead.

This fairly new Pacer unit, No. 142041, is about to leave Hooton station for Birkenhead in 1986. They were cheaply built, being based on the body of a Leyland National bus, for a relatively short life. Who would have thought Northern would still be running this unit in 2018?

During June 1986 I was working in Wales. I stopped at Caersws station and took this shot of Sprinter No. 150136 heading for Shrewsbury. This unit is now working with Northern.

A contrast in shapes at Cardiff Central – the HST is ready to leave for London, while No. 08646 pottered around the station for half an hour with parcels vans.

A great reminder of the days when Class 37s ruled the rails on the West Highland line. No. 37424 is carrying a Highland terrier motif at Lochailort on 24 August 1987. (Tony Woof)

No. 47120 *RAF Kinloss* is double-heading another Class 47 northbound through Nuneaton on a coal train in June 1987.

A merry-go-round coal train moves through Nuneaton station on 17 April 1987 headed by the penultimate Class 58, No. 58049 *Littleton Colliery*. This engine was about four months old at the time I took this picture. The 58s were eclipsed by the General Motors imports (Class 59), which started to appear in 1986 and eventually consigned these ungainly looking Type 5 engines to the role of interesting sidelines.

This is an interesting train with car-carrying wagons. It is seen running southbound through Nuneaton in April 1987, hauled by Class 81 No. 81013.

Preserved 'Western' diesel D1041 *Western Prince* is seen on display at the Crewe works open day in July 1987. She was built at Crewe in 1962.

The future of freight – Class 59 No. 59002 *Yeoman Enterprise* passes Great Cheverell on 29 June 1987 with a westbound train of Foster Yeoman empties. The privatised train has arrived and this order for five engines led to further orders for hundreds of similar, but more powerful Class 66s. (Tony Woof)

You don't get too many really interesting trains any more – like this Brush Type 2, seen at Coventry with just two parcels vans in the evening sunshine in July 1987. The ubiquitous Class 310 unit waits to leave for Birmingham.

Sadly, the return to steam of A4 No. 4468 *Mallard* was a fairly brief affair, but here she looks superb running through Birkett Common on 27 August 1988. (Tony Woof)

Brand new at Liverpool Lime Street in October 1988 is Class 90 No. 90026 in Main Line livery, which was similar to InterCity but without the swallow motifs.

It was great to see this old Great Central veteran, 4-4-0 No. 506 *Butler-Henderson*, back in steam in the 1980s. In August 1988, she has arrived at Quorn station and is running round her train.

On 8 September 1988, Class K1 2-6-0 No. 2005 crosses Glenfinnan Viaduct on the West Highland line; a patch of sunlight illuminates the scene to create a dramatic picture. (Tony Woof)

At Lyndhurst Road station on 12 June 1988, No. 47379 *Total Energy* has a good load of tank wagons in tow. It is odd that a station in the New Forest, on the old London & South Western Railway, should be part of Network SouthEast.

A few old electric locomotives were retained at Willesden for empty stock work, their paintwork ravaged by years of chemical cleaning. They were Class 83 and 82 units and this is No. 82005, seen stabled on a short siding on the Up side just on the approach to Euston in June 1988.

Class 86/1 No. 86103 *André Chapelon* has just arrived at Liverpool Lime Street in October 1988. The recently applied livery, one of several variations of InterCity colours in use at the time, shows severe signs of wear.

A worthy body they may be, but the *Institution of Electrical Engineers* is hardly a name to excite passengers as No. 86407 waits to leave Coventry for Euston in April 1988.

This Class 47, No. 47592 *County of Avon*, is seen arriving at Exeter St David's station engine on a bright day in February 1988 with coaches in a mixture of liveries. The engine looks ex-works, but the stock does not match.

You may be old enough to remember that a three-car Birmingham RCW DMU Class 118 unit was painted in yellow British Telecom livery in the 1980s. Here it is seen arriving at Exeter St David's station in February 1988 as part of its rota of working Devon and Cornwall services. At the time, it caused quite a stir.

Having been repainted in original green livery, Class 33 No. 33008 *Eastleigh* is running light engine through Exeter St David's in February 1988 – a shame she wasn't cleaner. This engine has been preserved at the East Somerset Railway.

Among classes to sport the Network SouthEast colours were the Class 50s. Here, well west of London, is No. 50026 *Indomitable*, seen arriving at Reading. (Bob Mullins)

An immaculate Class 73/2 electro-diesel, No. 73208 *County of East Sussex*, is about to depart Victoria station with the UK part of the Venice–Simplon Orient Express in June 1988. Amazingly, it is still around, having been rebuilt as No. 73971 for Caledonian Sleeper duties.

Rugby's interesting, if rather ramshackle station is seen here as No. 86210 *City of Edinburgh* arrives on a Euston-bound train on 14 August 1988. Even after the Leamington, Peterborough and Leicester branches closed, Rugby still seemed extremely busy. Once it had huge yards and workshops, but until recent times it was always plagued by severe speed restrictions.

Class 47/3 No. 47347 – the freight version – enters Liverpool Lime Street on 12 October 1988 with an express from Newcastle. Note the sector colours, denoting the engine was allocated to metals workings. As the engine had no train heating, it may have been a chilly ride for passengers.

Class 73 No. 73138 *Post Haste* leads a sister locomotive on the South West Main Line through Lyndhurst Road (since renamed Ashurst New Forest) on 12 July 1988. The new Wessex Electrics, Class 442, were to soon take over.

Naming ceremonies have always attracted interest. On this occasion, electric No. 86401 in Network SouthEast livery is being christened *Northampton Town* at Northampton station in April 1989. (Bob Mullins)

AC Cars railbus SC79979. Just a body, it was dumped in the foliage at Boat of Garten station in April 1989 and was cut up three years later. Five of these units were built and sister unit W79978 is preserved.

In March 1989 a new Class 90 engine, No. 90005 *Financial Times,* in the latest InterCity livery passes through Northampton. (Bob Mullins)

Push-pull-fitted Class 47/7 diesel No. 47712 *Lady Diana Spencer* is seen at Aberdeen on 14 August 1989. The scruffy ScotRail livery hardly befits a royal princess, which is what she was at the time of this photograph.

Class 86/1 No. 86101 *Sir William A. Stanier F.R.S.* with parcels vans in March 1990 at Preston. The InterCity livery had several variations, this one featuring a full yellow front end. (Bob Mullins)

Passing construction works for the new A43 road bridge at Blisworth in the summer of 1990 is Class 87 No. 87004 *Britannia,* the new road obliterating much of the historic Blisworth to Peterborough line. In the 1980s, many once-useful routes – some with future potential – were lost through the rush to build new roads. *Britannia* is working the 'wrong line'.

A variety of motive power at Manchester Victoria in April 1990 with Sprinter No. 150111, a Class 31 and a Class 47 on show. (Bob Mullins)

A Class 86-hauled train heads south through Weedon, Northamptonshire, beneath a watery winter sun in February 1990.

The Class 89 electric locomotive was destined to remain an orphan. Designed by Brush and built at Crewe, No. 89001 *Avocet* was hardly a thing of great beauty and had two fairly short periods of service, after which it was preserved. Here, it hauls the 'Modern Railways 500' special at Sandy on 27 May 1990. (Richard Denny)

In one of many superb shots taken by Tony Woof on this route, Class 58 No. 58036 pilots No. 47456 along the Settle to Carlisle line on 3 March 1990 with the 08.25 from Leeds. (Tony Woof)

Bibliography

Evans, J., *Railways in Transition 1975–1985* (Stroud: Amberley Publishing, 2017).

Fox, P. and Webster N. (eds), *Motive Power Pocket Book* (Sheffield: Platform Five, 1979–1989).

Marsden, C. and Wood, R. (eds), *British Rail Motive Power, Combined Volume* (Shepperton: Ian Allan, 1976–1989).

Montague, K., *Westerns, Hymeks and Warships*, (Oxford: Oxford Publishing, 1975).

Peel, D., *Locomotive Headboards* (Stroud: Sutton Publishing, 2006).

Flickr: www.flickr.com (accessed 31 March 2018).

Southern Locomotives Ltd: http://www.southern-locomotives. co.uk/34072/34072_Restoration.html. (accessed 12 June 2018).

APT – With Hindsight by Professor Alan Wickens (2008): http://www. apt-p.com/APTWithHindsight.htm. (accessed 15 June 2018).

The Great Western Archive: http://www.greatwestern.org.uk/preserve. htm. (accessed May 15 2018).

Modern Railways (Weybridge: Ian Allan, February 1994).

Modern Railways Pictorial (Shepperton: Ian Allan).

Rail Magazine (Peterborough: EMAP Business Press).

Railway World (Shepperton: Ian Allan).

Railway Magazine (London: IPC Business Press).

Steam Railway (Peterborough: Bauer).